Sports Records

# Basketball Records

by Anthony K. Hewson

FOCUS READERS

BEACON

www.focusreaders.com



Focus Readers is distributed by North Star Editions:
sales@northstareditions.com | 888-417-0195

Produced for Focus Readers by Red Line Editorial.

Photographs ©: Ross D. Franklin/AP Images, cover, 1, 27; AP Images, 4, 7, 8–9, 10, 16, 29; G. Paul Burnett/AP Images, 13; Ben Margot/AP Images, 15; Gregory Vasil/CSM/Cal Sport Media/AP Images, 19; Mark J. Terrill/AP Images, 21; Jeff Chiu/AP Images, 22; Kathy Willens/AP Images, 25

**Library of Congress Cataloging-in-Publication Data**
Names: Hewson, Anthony K., author.
Title: Basketball records / by Anthony K. Hewson.
Description: Lake Elmo, MN : Focus Readers, 2021 | Series: Sports records | Includes index. | Audience: Grades 4-6
Identifiers: LCCN 2020002182 (print) | LCCN 2020002183 (ebook) | ISBN 9781644933602 (Hardcover) | ISBN 9781644934364 (Paperback) | ISBN 9781644935880 (PDF) | ISBN 9781644935125 (eBook)
Subjects: LCSH: Basketball--Records--Juvenile literature.
Classification: LCC GV885.1 .H48 2021 (print) | LCC GV885.1 (ebook) | DDC 796.323--dc23
LC record available at https://lccn.loc.gov/2020002182
LC ebook record available at https://lccn.loc.gov/2020002183

Printed in the United States of America
Mankato, MN
082020

## About the Author

Anthony K. Hewson is a freelance writer, originally from San Diego, now living in the Bay Area with his wife and their two dogs.

# Table of Contents

PHILA
13
Los Angeles
14
PHILA
5

## Chapter 1

# Wilt Hits 100

Wilt Chamberlain was on fire. His Philadelphia Warriors teammates kept passing him the ball. And Chamberlain kept making baskets. The year was 1962. The Warriors were playing the New York Knicks.

**Wilt Chamberlain scored more than 31,000 points during his career.**

Chamberlain racked up 41 points by halftime. In the third quarter he scored 28 more points. The Knicks started to **foul** him. They hoped to slow him down. But Chamberlain made 28 of his 32 **free throws**.

With 46 seconds left in the game, Chamberlain scored his

## Fun Fact

**The National Basketball Association (NBA) was not as popular in 1962 as it is today. Chamberlain's 100-point game wasn't shown on TV.**

**Wilt Chamberlain led the NBA in scoring for six seasons in a row.**

100th point. That game became legendary. It was the only time an NBA player scored in the triple digits.

# Wilt Power

Wilt Chamberlain's career numbers are impressive. And he may be best known for scoring 100 points in a game. But that record was part of an even more amazing season. In 1961–62, Chamberlain averaged 50.4 points per game.

James Harden was the scoring leader in 2018–19. But Harden only averaged 36.1 points. Even if Harden had scored 1,000 more points, he still would not have reached Chamberlain's average. Chamberlain is in a class by himself.

Chamberlain played for the Lakers for five seasons.

LAKERS
13

PHILA
13
6

Chapter 2

# Great Games

In 1960, Wilt Chamberlain and the Warriors faced the Boston Celtics. Bill Russell was a great defender for the Celtics. But not in this game. Chamberlain had 55 **rebounds**. That set a record.

**Bill Russell (6) played his entire career with the Boston Celtics.**

## Shot Blocker

Elmore Smith was known as "The Rejector." He was one of the best shot blockers in NBA history. In one game, Smith blocked 17 shots. That broke the old record of 14. Smith had set the old record himself just two days earlier.

**Fun Fact**

**Elmore Smith had 393 blocks during the 1973–74 season. That was the most in the NBA that season.**

**Elmore Smith (3) was a first-round pick in the 1971 NBA Draft.**

# Buckets and More Buckets

Klay Thompson has splashed in many **three-pointers** over the years. During a 2015 game, Thompson scored 37 points in the third quarter alone. That was a record. Thompson set another record when he made all nine of his three-pointers in that quarter. Thompson played for 33 minutes in the game. But he scored 52 points.

In 2018, Thompson (middle) broke the record for most three-pointers in a game with 14.

UCLA
32

Chapter 3

# Top Teams

The University of California Los Angeles (UCLA) has the longest winning **streak** in men's college basketball. In January 1971, the UCLA Bruins lost to Notre Dame. But they won their next game.

**Bill Walton (32) was a star center during UCLA's winning streak.**

And they kept on winning. The Bruins didn't lose again until 1974. Their streak ended at 88 games.

## Connecticut Can't Lose

In November 2014, the University of Connecticut women's team lost in overtime. They didn't lose again for 865 days. During that time, the Huskies won 111 games in a row. Those wins included two national titles.

The streak came to an end in 2017. The Huskies lost in overtime.

**Moriah Jefferson played point guard for the UConn Huskies during their winning streak.**

But they had the longest winning streak in the history of college basketball, men's or women's.

## Luck of the Irish

In the NBA, no team can match the Boston Celtics. As of 2019, the Celtics had 17 titles. That is the most titles of any NBA team.

The Celtics have also won the most championships in a row. They won every single title

**Fun Fact**

**Bill Russell won 11 championships with the Celtics. No player in NBA history has won more.**

**Kevin Garnett (5) led the Boston Celtics to a title in 2008.**

from 1959 to 1966. No other **professional** sports team in North America has matched that streak.

Rakuten
WARRIORS
SPALDING

Chapter 4

# Super Seasons

Stephen Curry's name is all over the NBA record books. In 2012–13, he scored 272 three-pointers. That was a new record. But Curry was not finished. In 2014–15, he broke his own record by scoring 286.

**Stephen Curry has one of the highest three-point percentages in NBA history.**

Then in 2015–16, he smashed the record. Curry drained an amazing 402 three-pointers that season.

**Fun Fact**

**Through 2018–19, Curry held 5 of the top 10 spots for most three-pointers in a season.**

## Triple Threat

It takes a special player to average a **triple-double** for a season. The player must be great at scoring,

**Russell Westbrook looks for an open teammate in a game against the New York Knicks.**

passing, and rebounding. Oscar Robertson did it first in 1961–62. In 2016–17, Russell Westbrook became the second player to do it.

Westbrook averaged another triple-double the next season. And in 2018–19, he made it three seasons in a row.

## Point Machine

Diana Taurasi started playing in the Women's National Basketball Association (WNBA) in 2004. In 2006, she scored 860 points. That was a new single-season scoring record.

Taurasi is the league's all-time leading scorer. And in 2018, she

**As of 2019, Diana Taurasi had won three WNBA titles with the Phoenix Mercury.**

was the first player in WNBA history to reach 8,000 career points.

FOCUS ON

# Basketball Records

*Write your answers on a separate piece of paper.*

1. Write a letter to a friend explaining what you learned about Wilt Chamberlain's 100-point game.
2. Which basketball record do you think is the most impressive? Why?
3. Who was the first player to make 400 three-pointers in a season?
   - A. Wilt Chamberlain
   - B. Stephen Curry
   - C. James Harden
4. Which player holds the record for most triple-double seasons in a row?
   - A. Klay Thompson
   - B. Kevin Garnett
   - C. Russell Westbrook

**5.** What does **legendary** mean in this book?

*That game became **legendary**. It was the only time an NBA player scored in the triple digits.*

**A.** well-known
**B.** a high number
**C.** easy to forget

**6.** What does **splashed in** mean in this book?

*Klay Thompson has **splashed in** many three-pointers over the years. During a 2015 game, Thompson scored 37 points in the third quarter alone.*

**A.** scored
**B.** fouled
**C.** lost

*Answer key on page 32.*

# Glossary

**foul**
To break the rules of a game.

**free throws**
Shots from the foul line worth one point each, given to a team after one of its players has been fouled.

**professional**
Paid to do something as a job, rather than doing it just for fun.

**rebounds**
Plays in which a player controls the ball after a missed shot.

**streak**
When something happens many times in a row.

**three-pointers**
Shots made from beyond the three-point line on a basketball court.

**triple-double**
A game in which a player has double-digit numbers in three categories. The categories are often points, assists, and rebounds.

# To Learn More

## BOOKS

Adamson, Thomas K. *Basketball Records.* Minneapolis: Bellwether Media, 2018.

Frederick, Shane. *Basketball's Record Breakers.* North Mankato, MN: Capstone Press, 2017.

Mason, Tyler. *Incredible Basketball Records.* Mankato, MN: Child's World, 2016.

## NOTE TO EDUCATORS

Visit **www.focusreaders.com** to find lesson plans, activities, links, and other resources related to this title.

# Index



**Answer Key: 1.** Answers will vary; **2.** Answers will vary; **3.** B; **4.** C; **5.** A; **6.** A